# A Children's Zoo

## by Tana Hoban

Greenwillow Books, New York

Library of Congress
Cataloging in Publication Data

Hoban, Tana.
A children's zoo.
Summary: Color photographs of
animals are accompanied by
several descriptive words, e.g.
tall, spotted, silent giraffe.
1. Animals—Juvenile literature.
[1. Animals] I. Title.
QL49.H674   1985
591      84-25318
ISBN 0-688-05202-9
ISBN 0-688-05204-5 (lib. bdg.)

Especially for Kirk and Oliver

# black
# white
# waddles

# PENGUIN

big
smooth
swims

# HIPPOPOTAMUS

# striped
# black and white
# gallops

# ZEBRA

white
big
growls

POLAR BEAR

# sleek
# black
# swims

# SEA LION

strong
shaggy
roars

LION

red
blue
squawks

PARROT

# gray
# wrinkled
# trumpets

# ELEPHANT

black
white
furry

PANDA

spotted
silent

GIRAFFE

# A Children's Zoo

| | | Where do they come from? | Where do they live? | What do they eat? |
|---|---|---|---|---|
| PENGUINS | | Antarctica, Australia, Africa, South America, New Zealand, Galapagos Islands | by the sea | fish |
| HIPPOPOTAMUSES | | Africa | near rivers and swamps | vegetation |
| ZEBRAS | | Africa | in woods and mountains | vegetation |
| POLAR BEARS | | the Arctic | on ice floes and shores | fish and meat |
| SEA LIONS | | the Pacific and Atlantic Oceans | on ice floes and shores | fish |
| LIONS | | Africa, Asia | on the plains | meat |
| PARROTS | | Africa, Asia, Australia, New Zealand | in jungles | vegetation |
| ELEPHANTS | | Africa, Asia | in forests and on the plains | vegetation |
| PANDAS | | Asia | in forests and mountains | vegetation and meat |
| GIRAFFES | | Africa | in the bush | vegetation |
| KODIAK BEARS (cover) | | North America | in the Northern wilderness | fish and meat |